Why not share?

By Janine Amos and Annabel Spenceley
Consultant Rachael Underwood

CHERRYTREE BOOKS

A Cherrytree Book

Designed and produced by A S Publishing
Design and typesetting by James Leaman and Michael Leaman

First published 2000
by Cherrytree Press
327 High Street
Slough
Berkshire
SL1 1TX

A subsidiary of the Evans Publishing Group

Copyright © Evans Brothers Limited 2000

British Library Cataloguing in Publication Data
Amos, Janine
Why not share? – (Problem solvers)
1. Sharing. Juvenile Literature
I. Title II. Spenceley, Annabel
302. 1'4

ISBN 1 842 34026 3

Printed in Italy by G. Canale & C. S.p.A. - Turin

All rights reserved. No part of this publication may be reproduced,
stored in a retrieval system, or transmitted in any form or by any
means, electronic, mechanical, photocopying or otherwise, without the
prior permission in writing of the publishers.

Why not share?

Sometimes you and your friends may want different things. That could be a problem – but you can learn to work it out together. Here are some steps to help you.

 First of all, let everyone say how they feel

 Say what the problem is

 Talk about different ways to solve the problem

 Then choose a way that makes everyone happy

The children in this book all help each other to solve problems and share with each other. As you read, see if you can follow the problem-solving steps they use.

Megan's brainwave

Lunch is finished. Some children run out with a ball.

"Come on! I'll be in goal!" calls Nathan.
Michel kicks the ball hard. Theo heads it to Ben. They
rush all over the playground.
  "To me! To me!" yells Nathan.

Liam, Megan and Holly go outside too.
"Let's play tag," says Liam. "Who'll be it?"

Liam and Megan chase Holly. Just then, Nathan's ball lands – crash – in the middle of their game.
"Sorry!" calls Ben. "Goal kick to me!"

Liam, Megan and Holly carry on playing. Then the football hits Megan on her head. It hurts.

"Look what you've done!" shouts Holly.

"Get out of our way, then!" Nathan shouts back.
"We're in the middle of a game!"

Everyone is feeling upset.

"They've taken over all the space," Megan complains.

"Shall we play something else, over in the corner?" suggests Liam.

"No, why should we?" says Holly crossly. "It's a problem. It needs sorting out."

Holly asks Mrs Casey for help. The boys stop their game and come over, too.

"Can you tell me what the problem is?" asks the teacher.

"We're just playing football," explains Theo.
"There's no space for us to play!" says Holly.

"How can you all share this space?" asks Mrs Casey. "Any ideas?"

"We could all play football!" suggests Nathan.
"No!" shout Holly and Theo.

Megan is thinking hard.

"How about a chalk line?" she says at last. "We draw a line on the ground – football on one side and tag on the other!"

"The ball will bounce over sometimes!" says Michel, frowning.

"Sometimes is OK," laughs Holly.

"Let's try it!" says Nathan, running to get some chalk.

Later, Mrs Casey checks to see how the idea is working. Holly gives her a thumbs-up sign. At the same time, Michel scores a goal!

Planting the garden

The class is working in the school garden. Mrs Casey shows the children how to dig over the ground with a fork.
She shows them how to put a plant carefully in the soil.
"Now it's your turn," she says to the children.

Alice, Tom and Liam work quickly. Alice digs over the soil. Tom and Liam do the planting. Soon they have planted six primroses!

Sita and Michel plant slowly. They are careful not to damage any roots.

Sita and Michel pick up their second plant.
"Where shall we put it?" asks Michel.
"There, by the path?" suggests Sita.
"Tom and Liam have already planted there," says
Michel.

"Here, then?" says Sita.
"They've been there too – look!" Michel tells her.

Sita steps backwards.
"Mind out!" calls Alice. "We're working here!"

Michel sits down.
"There's no space left!" he sighs.

"Let's talk to the others. Let's sort it out," says Sita. "Come on!"

She goes over to Alice, Tom and Liam.

"There's no room for us," she tells them. "You're using all the garden!"

"We didn't mean to!" Tom tells her.

"We need a plan," says Sita. "We all need to say where we'll plant – before we do it."

"OK," agrees Liam. "You have that part – all along the wall. We'll keep to this side."

Alice and Tom nod.

"OK," smiles Michel.

By lunchtime, all the plants are in.
"Look what we've done!" the children say proudly.
They show their garden to Mrs Casey.

When there's a problem

When you and your friends are playing or working together, it is sometimes easy to forget about others.
Sometimes you may take over all the space and forget to share. Other people may feel upset.

If anyone is getting upset, there is a problem. Stop what you are doing and talk about it. Try to sort out the problem together. Work out a way for everyone to use the space happily.

Problem Solving

The children in Mrs Casey's class solved their problems. They remembered a few problem-solving ideas:

 Let everyone say how they feel

 Share information about what happened and let everyone say what they want

 Be clear about what the problem is

 Talk about different ideas for sorting out the problem

 Agree on an idea together – and try it out!

This plan might help you next time you have a problem to solve. Sometimes a problem may seem too big to tackle alone. You might need to talk about it with an adult first.